T0413370

What Can You Get?

Consultants

Ashley Bishop, Ph.D.
Sue Bishop, M.E.D.

Publishing Credits

Dona Herweck Rice, *Editor-in-Chief*
Robin Erickson, *Production Director*
Lee Aucoin, *Creative Directo*
Tim J. Bradley, *Illustrator Manager*
Chad Thompson, *Illustratorr*
Sharon Coan, *Project Manager*
Jamey Acosta, *Editor*
Rachelle Cracchiolo, M.A.Ed., *Publisher*

Teacher Created Materials

5301 Oceanus Drive
Huntington Beach, CA 92649-1030
http://www.tcmpub.com
ISBN 978-1-4333-2941-8
© 2012 Teacher Created Materials, Inc.
Printed in China
Nordica.082019.CA21901019

I can get a pen.

I can get a mug.

I can get a pop.

I can get a cut.

I can get a bug.

I can get a pot.

I can get a nut.

I can get a hug.

What can you get

Glossary

bug	**cut**
hug	**mug**
nut	**pen**
pop	**pot**

Sight Words

I   can   get   a
What   you

Extension Activities

Read the story together with your child. Use the discussion questions before, during, and after your reading to deepen your child's understanding of the story and the rime (word family) that is introduced.

The activities provide fun ideas for continuing the conversation about the story and the vocabulary that is introduced. They will help your child make personal connections to the story and use the vocabulary to describe prior experiences.

Discussion Questions
- Why would you need a pen?
- What goes into a mug?
- Have you ever had a cut?
- Do you like bugs?

Activities at Home
- Walk around the house and have your child get three things down from shelves. Ask your child to draw a picture of one of the things.
- Have your child put together a small first-aid kit to use if he or she gets a cut.